Mr. Bluebird

Mr. Bluebird

Gerry Gomez Pearlberg

THE UNIVERSITY OF WISCONSIN PRESS

The University of Wisconsin Press
1930 Monroe Street
Madison, Wisconsin 53711

www.wisc.edu/wisconsinpress/

3 Henrietta Street
London WC2E 8LU, England

5   4   3   2   I

Printed in the United States of America

Library of Congress Cataloging-in-Publication Data
Pearlberg, Gerry.
   Mr. Bluebird / Gerry Gomez Pearlberg.
   p. cm.
   ISBN 0-299-19324-I (alk. paper)
I. Title.
PS3566.E2183M7   2003
811'.54—dc21   2003045833

TABLE OF CONTENTS

Making My Move	3
Flicker	4
Monroe	5
The Moment You've Been Waiting For	7
Another Story	8
Processional	11
Free Looking	14
Springs	16
Portrait of a Neighbor's Tree in Bloom	19
Camperdown Elm	22
Birding Update	24
Futurity	25
Event	28
Down	29
From the St. Francis Sonnets	30
Migration	30
Alchemy	31
Succession	32
"A Bird in the Body it Came With"	33
Regeneration	34
Dislodging Esperanza	35
Smokestack Seen from the Air	36
Industrial Trinity	37
Dream Extraction	38
Muse Prescriptions	40
Things I Question	41
Heavens to Mergatroid!	42
City of Suchness	44
Predictions	47
Dead Constellation	50

From the St. Augustine Sonnets 51
   Thirst 51
   Pact 52
   Admission 53
   Thy Creature 54
   The Death & Life of Paul Bowles 55
A Chance of Snow Later 56
Untitled Stations 57
Mr. Eggroll 58
Goodbye Mr. Chips 62
New Italian Cinema (Napoli Dust) 67
What Movie Not to See 69
Paint 70
Transubstantiation 71
For You, Anything 73
Cling 74
Somewhere in Wistconsin 75
Fin de Fiesta 76
   1: candela 76
   2: cascada 77
   3: espina 78
   4: llamarada 79
   5: Dhammapada 80
Ghost-Mattress 81
A Troubled Mind 83
My Tumulus 84
Equipoise 85
Litany At Dusk 87
Climbing Yesterday 89
Inside the Hour 94
Betsy McCall 98

Acknowledgments 101
About the Author 103

Mr. Bluebird

MAKING MY MOVE

There will be no incident to describe

Just a foot sinking deeper into its shoe

And the shoe into the mudflat of its salty way

I have involved myself with little somethings

For so long

That part of me has gone back to them

Language is loosening its grip

Phosphorescent shrimp-crickets leaping

On the mudflat at dusk

Spell only themselves

The flat wrinkled balloons of sea creatures

Stranded in sand are soft

I walk barefoot among them

I am an out-going tide

    an out-going tide

You wouldn't know me if you saw me

FLICKER

The flicker, in its redness,
watches from its high, dead branch.
It cocks its head and shows
its black-and-white back, yes
there are hyphens between its black and whiteness.

The streambed is blanketed
with dead leaves, blades of dead
and living grass, and here
and there a crushed beer can
enveloped in a fine brown pelt of velvet silt.

From time to time (and I have all of it now),
a dead leaf rolls by underwater
spinning against the current that propels it
as if trying to leap backward.

These leaves are ochre stags –
shot through with autumn: cloven
hoof, tendon, shoulder wound, stem:
hindquarters thrashing in the current's hail
of quicksilver arrows, its bone-and-
blood-specked foam, its panicky whirlpools.

   At the surface of the stream, a bare, bow-shaped branch
   floats in place, taking aim.

   The water, gliding around it, flickers in an arc from its edges,
   as if to illustrate its tension.

   The odd thing
   is that nothing
   holds the floating branch in place,
   and that it keeps shooting, shooting
   though it has no bowstring.

MONROE

Molly's covered in algae
rubbed in muskrat residue.
Let's bring the cameras to the pond
to nab those colors while we can.
It's almost gruesome here
in the ostrichy morning light
for Autumn has not yet tipped its
glinting flask. It's only started trickling
its oils and grand combustions.

Today
I'm Aladdin, or something
along those lines, switching places
with the idea of myself as un-
encumbered, adventurous, free.

A ravenous Questionmark
plops onto the thistle.
She puts her nose in the hole
and it's flecked with specks of emerald –
what summer gave up fighting for.
There's a perfect hole in the algae
where some mammal head popped
up and plunked back down again
but soon the spot refills with green.

The joy
of rolling
in grass in grass
cannot be disproved by any science:
it fills itself in,
gnawing the wet log
and spitting out the woody flecks with pride.
The rummaging cry of a woodpecker
high in the trees might possibly

be pileated –
              but who is that lucky?

A spider has
dropped
like an earring
from my ear –
an omen everyone remarks on,
and under their admiring phrases
I preen, so enjoying my slice
of chocolate-yellow birthday
cake in the sun
on the lawn
that for the time being
it seems everything's under control:
pileated. I spit out
summer's green and bitter bark
in grand gestures. I stand
erect at the edge of the bracken,
saluting the world with my orangina spots –
there's one for every year of living,
and this year we're even.
Red efts tumble from
my lymph nodes
for I am in a maple-y mood.
Above (of course) perch vultures with outstretched wings,
flying in place on the breezy electric wires
and believe me, it's worth it.

The old train moves nonstop across the tressel
without a trace of restlessness.
It's this I'm risking it all for.

THE MOMENT YOU'VE BEEN WAITING FOR

Two dogs volley-bark back and forth.
That book you admire has won the Pulitzer.
A young magpie hops from branch to branch,
balancing with its tail
                         but your legs are crossed,
your shoe half-slipping from your foot,
barely balanced.
Cool air glides beneath your arch, along the heel, within the toes.
You think of fleet-footed Mercury
with his wingéd high-tops and forkéd tongue.
There is nothing fleet-footed about you.
The air smells like the rain that never did arrive.
All day, this cloudful sky just going from one thing to another.
A horsefly paws the dandelion flower
so crammed with yellow it's inside out.
The lawn is full of them, brisk and eager.
The young magpie clambers into his enormous hive.
Hidden in that waffled chamber, he
resolutely rehearses his wavering call:
muffled yet available,
like the tenuous inflections
of a once-essential god,
now all but forgotten
in purpose and in name,
sequestered,
perplexed by his state,
but practicing his incantations daily, just in case.

ANOTHER STORY

I am photographing the grave markers in this campo santo –
sheet metal, splintered wood, and boulders hauled up from the field,
on which the names of the deceased are inscribed
with thumb tacks and turquoise paint,
lovingly adorned with inexpensive, useful things.

There is a perfect view of the mountain from here,
more fervent than any other vantage point
in articulating the mountain's omnipotence.

On one of the burial mounds lies a half-buried can of Hills
Brothers Coffee: decaffeinated, family-sized,
intended as a floral vase. Now, emptied of flowers
and inclining toward earth, it's become a joke or riddle.

There are many flowers here, all wild and purple.

I'm trying to get beyond nature, color,
architecture, birds. But they're what I love.
And I desperately need this slow and careful practice
of trying to really see this life, and trying to say it.

It's made me a stickler for details –
the illegible, eroded, the rubbed-out and rotted.
Everything that cowers on the edge of being forgotten.

After all these years it's affected my memory –
parts of my mind diminishing
in deference to others, as rock recedes to lichen
and then again to moss.

At this point, it's beyond my control.
I make note of it, try to move on.

It's a race to see who'll move on first.
I hope it's me.
Because I don't want to be
around to see what happens
if it turns out to be you.

There's only so much mystique a person can take.
I should've said that at the start.
I do like this nice mountain
and the shrieking kids in the distance,
their instability and delight.
That lawn mower, even, at proper volume,
eight lawns away and spewing the exhilarating smell
of newly cut grass throughout this graveyard.
I hope I'm not disturbing anyone here by taking
these snapshots and writing this poem.
I think you'd be surprised to learn
that two whole tombstones bear your name.
I know I was. I read the word over and over
and was very disturbed to suddenly find myself
so close. It's something I normally
try to avoid. But these days, there's always some-
body about – hanging laundry or whatnot –
it's hard to be alone when out-of-doors.
It must be hard on the mountain.
Now that the snow has melted – just traces remain –
it looks so much softer, but just as distinguished.

Guess I'll take a photograph of that before I go –
mountainous
backdrop to the turquoise
cross at the cemetery gate marked
Take Your Trash and Boxes With You.
The dead and living share this lack
of please-and-thank-you's.

I'm just not well.
Lord knows you've borne
the brunt of that a thousand times before.
Take heart, take heart.
In 24 hours it will all be different.
In 24 hours it always is.

[Campo Santo de Nuestros Padre Jesús de Nazareno, Taos]

PROCESSIONAL

Names - Common Dandelion; Blowball; Lion's-tooth; Peasant's Clock.

Flower-head - Solitary, golden yellow, 1 to 2 in. across containing 150 to 200 perfect ray florets on a flat receptacle at the top of a hollow, milky scape 2 to 18 in. tall.

Leaves - From a very deep, thick, bitter root.

Preferred Habitat - Lawns, fields, grassy waste places.

Flowering Season - Every month of the year.

Distribution - Around the civilized world.

Is it, is it, is
it the siskins?
It is, it is, it
is the siskins!
A flock of 'em,
sounds like,
but not one
can be seen
from this
"grassy waste place,"
here among
the dandelions
(of which siskins
make mincemeat
when not concealed
in trees). Dozens
of siskins have
recently arrived,
following the
dandelions as
the dandelions
go to seed. The
contest is on:
Yellow Zealots

and their parachute-
seeded spheres
openly vying
for the field:
"It's Smoke-
Bubbles vs.
Plunging Yellow"
and the word
is indeed spreading –
    via wind which lifts the parachutes away
    and via
    Orange Sulphurs and Checkered Whites
    who deign to land
    on brightnesses beyond them
    extending slow proboscises:::::::::::::::::::::::::::::::::sip, sip, sip.

Common dandelion
tilting beneath such
unabashed carnival-
yellow health, you
really *do* wear the face
of ripeness, crown
of enthusiasm
the field endures proudly,
processional for a monarch.
Who else is fit to preside
over this or any other
civilized field – who
more abundant, more
generous, cheerful,
persistent, unassuming –
what other bitter root yields
such pervasive joy and vigor?
Humble without meekness,
you have filled and fluffed

this acreage with seed
and gold coinage.
The ground erupts with yellow
as the air erupts
with the disembodied buzz
of siskins. Soon
they will descend en masse,
and tear apart
your blowball orbs,
spitting out
the downy tufts
(which vireos line
their nests with)
to reach the nourishing seeds
which mirror
in perfect miniature
the tawny breast-
stripes of siskins.

This remarkable resemblance between bird and seed –
compactness, marking, coloration –
sets into motion mysterious transactions,
for the moment the siskins descend
from their invisible perches to feed –
the moment they suspend their singing –

    the air takes on an extra weight,

    and turns the volume way, way up
    on dandelion-yellow wavelengths.

For Karen Cook, her birthday, May 1999.

Free Looking

"In my best moments I think 'life has passed me by'...." — *Agnes Martin*

I'm out
doing the
day.
Clouds
pass
in & out
in armloads –
some laundry.
How many
hours have I
wasted in
efficiency?
No, don't
tell me. Now
I want
only
to watch this –
this this or that
(it does not matter
what) –
crumble
or open
or swallow
something
else
preferably
something
much larger
than itself. I'm
here
& for

the moment
close
to happy
insular &
free.

SPRINGS

the colors drop out
of the nodding buds
like jujubes,
pulling away
from their stations
of green. Brooklyn
is backing its way
into yellows &
purples, pure
arrogance & bright.
a crocus shakes
an angry fist
at winter's frail,
translucent skull,
jerking hard
the cruel & royal
reins to send
those horse teeth packing.

what's it like to turn the book
& find yourself a page?
that's the story of spring,
& it's not "about" anything
any more than Brooklyn is,
though spring makes me
think of croaking –
there *were*, after all,
toads in the garden
on Bergen Street: that
must have been a miracle.
death's the unpatented
gizmo built into all real beauty:
the bones beneath the plush

exterior, spring velour: we love it
'cause we know
it ends. I spend
a fair amount
of mental time
on growing old
& getting old – the differences. & then
becoming old,
a whole other
can of worms.
I like to imagine the City –
half spore, half void, so much packed in –
drained out from under me
by time's seepage,
the place entirely changed.
I like to imagine my friends
& me as ghosts
revisiting the clock tower,
the gardens,
Eastern Parkway,
facing the fact that
even shared memories
can't hold it still, this vivid
lizard in constant re-
camouflage.

I think in death I'd find that sweet as soda through a paper straw
    that soon grows limp:

a comforting sense of flux & finitude
in red-n-white stripes. unlike
the cyberspace horizons
of today or one-hundred-years-next-Thursday.
I hope real books will still exist
by then, when time – nearsighted,
unlicensed driver – will surely have backed
into itself at breakneck speed

& come up short
insurance-wise.
a book is pleasure in the hand,
a whiff of flesh & look
the way it folds & bends
& breathes,
its spine & spores
& meat & gills
a mushroom sponge –
these are its properties & ours:
spatial, physical, finite:
the very essence of reading
& understanding
in this, the present world.
books end.
endings orient us.
& so I do wish books
on the citizens
of the future,
just as I wish on them
the onset of age,
memory its ranch & saddle,
its slow hoop of lasso over-winding the sky like a clock. because I like
the idea of oldness
being something
you can get
& that gets you.
& I do
love books,
at least in part
for the dread & relief
of knowing
they end.

for Stephanie Gilman

Portrait of a Neighbor's Tree in Bloom

It's holding redness
over its shoulders,
the neighbor's tree,
and dangling its tight red blooms
by their feet to make them scream
and scream.
This red
vacillates between
panic and tranquility,
each bud an anarchy.
Taken together,
it's more a debate
than a tree,
a conversation of,
by, for, and about
a certain red demeanor
imparting the classical quality
of old-world Japan –
but no, it's fuller, really,
a bit more hearty,
more, I think, Chinese.
But don't think
red lacquer.
Let's look at it
another way.
Transposed to words or phrases,
these buds say *popling, bobolink,* or *bite your tongue.*

Two dogs and a truck sleep in the shade of its red racket.

How does this compare, say, to a holiday
ribbon or carnival tent?
Equally intrusive but far more

somber. This is a red that repudiates
the very idea of ripeness
in favor of quieter
sophistications.
It *is* stand-offish.
It does not strain forth like other reds.
This is why lipsticks the world over
strive to emulate it:
though vigorous, it does not stoop
to showy candor or cheap display.
It keeps its secrets secret.
Mentally self-sufficient,
consciously and unconsciously red,
it knows well the value
of insularity and discretion and
embodies these erotic potentials.
It maintains this stance amidst
complete awareness
of the entire spectrum
available to it
and from that array
this particular version has been
arrived upon. One does not
reach this kind of red by chance,
red of a very winning checker.

Over the years, with the comings
and goings of searching seasons,
this tree has come to believe
that IT is the reason
the sun delays its setting in May
and this conviction has thickened its will.
The willows that surround it
are helpless to disprove it.
They are, in truth, outranked by this stout

red general of a tree
whose diminutive radiance
renders their tentative, almost
greasy-looking greens
a public embarrassment.
The red tree has no use whatsoever
for the frailty of these towering ferns,
disdainfully upstaging everything around it
while feigning utter indifference
to the half-finished utterances of wind
which make the willows shudder.
It remains unmoved
by everything but its own color.

O little tree, you must get weary
beneath your burden of red.

CAMPERDOWN ELM

Big news. I've finally encountered the Camperdown Elm
under the right conditions – you really have to see it
without its leaves, stepping boldly across its ginger nodules.
O God, don't take this sun away, this second chance
across whose pond I drag a stick
as if to score. Ten seconds before
Total Darkness:
would you like me to attach a name
to that blue?
Mallard's Throat, my gift to you.
It runs away with itself, porous with diamonds
that blue.
The energy here is particulate,
a forever-shifting shadow.
It covers you, leaves
you naked, a flannel shirt to
button and unsnap, picture perfect
as the light secluded in a rabbit's ear,
pink trough, quivering as anything
so sequestered must surely quiver:
the listening light,
Tiffany pink
of a rabbit's ear-ness: cherry blossom
coming and going the exact same moment: dumb
mammal confusion.
That's what makes the jackrabbit
the closest thing to a human being
when you see it in person,
the next best thing.
Because only stillness separates the one from the other,
and stillness is a thing of increment.
By which I mean: Thank you for helping me
get through this winter. This winter

and this fall.
Now the rabbit (where the azalea bushes used to be but aren't)
dematerializes –
quickly, quietly,
a ghost-dancer in the leaves.
Above which the trees are reading
the sunlight for a clue or message,
a message or a clue,
raising their lenses to the light,
smoothing out the old instructions.

BIRDING UPDATE

They're evening
grosbeaks not
bobolinks.
Could it be
the siskins
are becoming
yellower?
I think they are.
A tree swallow's flight:
sheer elegance.
"Separate Liquid Notes."
Sanderlings
spring inexplicably
to mind.
MacGillivray's
song simply undulates
upward. Yesterday's
shy black and orange:
Bullock's Oriole?
Baltimore?
The book says
they hybridize.
But now I think
it might have been
a black-headed
grosbeak.
Who was
MacGillivray?

for Karen, after Schuyler

FUTURITY

"Now I'm tranquil – I know I'm going from marvel to marvel." – Genet

I love lying around
waiting for the end
of day, growing weak
and dehydrated
while the sun, that
registered nurse,
dabs my face with
her clean warm towel.
She seeps through
my cotton pants,
sting-kissing the back
of my thigh.
O vivid, unofficial joy,
this stretching out
alongside sunlight
and the stretched-
out afternoon, alone
where cars drone
only in the distance
of other roads,
implying the lives
of people on their way.
Now is the time
when the whole day stiffens,
taking its temperature,
rectally. It stands at
attention, its hours
peaking. The trials
and dilemmas, deficits
and extra-credits
that so animated the hours

wither to detached
bemusement. The
day is a patient
returning from a great
fever, lonesome soul
in search of further
loneliness. The evening
meal may now
be contemplated
and soon will come
the coming in from
out-of-doors. All that
has gone wrong or
right this day
shall return to the shelf
like the mislabeled
prescription it is.
Amateur Hour
is officially over.
An unprecedented
sunset looms, a long-
held belief. Feelings
eavesdrop on one another,
stealing each other's
bright little pills.
Certain categories of effort,
among them light and heat,
suspend. Now comes
a new set of installations:
cooling air, lengthening
shadows in grass,
more sinuous
quiet. In late afternoon,
things get serious,
shaping up. Thoughts

reverse direction,
traveling not *from*
the mind but towards
it. The expenditure
of energy shifts from
punishment of thought
(that hamster wheel)
to more ecumenical
concerns. From this
gratifying distance
we examine and
diagnose the day,
looking forward
to the intervening
hours between
dinnertime
and dawn
before impaling
ourselves on
tomorrow's prognosis.

EVENT

after Braque

In this last
charcoaled blue light
it is the space between
the trees that makes
the trees. This cotton-
wood stand is stood
on end by light descending
the textured trunks. Riverine,
final, darkness grinds
the details to a somber, granular
blue. The tactile space between
trunks and branches unnerves the trees,
and the blue night, a precinct, finishes them off.

DOWN

Here's where the barbed wire
has failed entirely, struck down
by wiry brambles in their red and yellow heat.

What doesn't Nature carry downward?
Clouds give up their guests of blue weather.
Insects evict themselves from slipshod skins.
Silvery catkins slip from branch-tips like snails eclipsing.
Day ejects night like squid ink.
Night ejaculates day.

Who or what are these blue-leafed trees,
and why are they too falling?

FROM THE ST. FRANCIS SONNETS

MIGRATION

From his cell   he sees it
emptiness of his life thus far   moth riveted to a screen
the eyes on its wings   forever blank pried open: a perfect zero.
Prayer. Solitude.   Solitude. Prayer.
The mind de-boning   its plush mirage.
Hours talking   with his horse
while crossing the Umbrian   Plain. An encounter
with a leper in which   the mind is changed.
Fasting among beggars   stealing daddy's good velvet.
The horse's name?   Unknown.
To God he said   "Send me where I shall be."
Plunging hot pokers   in the mind's blue jelly.
Migration. Tenacity. Free   will. Trade. "Send me
where I shall be," he said   and named his empty horse *I'm Lost.*

ALCHEMY

First the part that comes before
the early years when wolves
the first few steps of any equation
which the hours went rushing
in intervals of suffering
the church's marble steps
to glisten. In those years the zero
weaknesses, steps to be ascended
Only later would uncertainty
up close, under the influence
upper echelons of a new equation
elaborate zeros, ornately carved
meant to be given
inconsequentially rich

the ornithology and wolves –
were still mythology and only
held water: aqueducts through
silencing all that swam them
joy. From a certain distance
seemed wet and meant
seemed simple, a merit of
on one's knees.
finally let him see those steps
of small-town wolves and birds,
purer mathematics   more
like an altar's silver ringlets –
transformed like ore:
to unabashedly poor.

SUCCESSION

Once, in a certain remote place
and spent his evening there
An unanswerable storm
to branches
around him   until he knew
argument. *Terror as I had never*
my shield in sequences
the tender leaf
unfolds then takes itself
impaled with violent blooms.
in thorns and fistfuls
leaves it grasping
Hungering.
Struck open.

he climbed a solitary tree
"to come to know a tree."
came on. He clung
as night branched down
he was part of a much larger
known which pierced
like love, as when
you've crumpled in your hand
away from you in fire
Love comes
cuts the hand and
its most radiant postures:
Humbled.
Felled.

"A Bird in the Body it Came With"

Two nights. Two dreams
twin birds attack
but fail to kill it.
of flesh torn from its torso
in her mouth, real as the stitches
Next, a hawk attacks
piercing it with its beak
of a warm-blooded
imposed poverty of her sleep
half-hearted imprints
Where are they off to?
"Never again the heart
the words she wakes up to.
A bird

of falconry. First,
an airborne dog
The dog careens to earth, a map
and Francis can taste that blood
she dreams and dreams.
and re-attacks a branch
as if seeking the pulse
answer. Above the self-
shooting stars carve
on the night.
It seems significant.
absent of birds" are
Day's simpler rephrasing:
in the body it came with.

REGENERATION

Soon thereafter, a woman
a saw whet owl looking on.
with a series of experiments –
by the long stone wall
field. Small trees grow against
something. They become
In late afternoon
them in soft duplicate
He breaks off branch
of each stolen limb remains
This episode never appears
nor, for political reasons
The limb removed
He'll spend his life

shows him something in a tree,
To which he replies
he'll call them "studies" –
dividing church and
the wall's edge, stunted by
his subjects.
the sun casts
along the moss-blue wall.
after branch yet the shadow
even waves.
in his personal writings
in any of the histories.
the shadow enduring.
discovering what it means.

DISLODGING ESPERANZA

after the demolition of a community garden, NYC, 2000

It's strange.
Days resemble
other days
& nothing keeps
track of them.

Today, the Mayor's bulldozers
bullied the hollow winter reeds,
dislodging Esperanza.

The people who love this garden have spent the night in jail
for defending what took twenty years to grow,
two hours to fell.

The dried cockscomb
dumped from its container
severed from its brain-stem
is a honey-golden mind

push-buzzing its questions to the etherized hive:

> *Define esperanza.*
> *Define civilized.*

SMOKESTACK SEEN FROM THE AIR

mountain shafts and wrinkles, hills as far as vision goes,
landscape of chins and pine-blue stubble: is it Pennsylvania's

five o'clock shadow we're flying over or Virginia's rustic jawbone?
distinct in the middle distance: one white smokestack

beside a dim river bend of skink-tail blue, a vertical
nick on the dimpled terrain as brittle as all the giant toys of men

when viewed from the air. its emissions gleam pink in the early evening
light, its salmon mane drifts skyward and is sternly bent back

so that now it's clear which way the wind is blowing. it forms
a wide, flat pelt of smoke, chivalrously laid across the river's anarchy

for some elegant and anonymous stiletto heel to trod upon
crossing back from all that can be trusted

to be true. whose hand will that elegant someone take
as he, she, or it – tipsily balanced on the prongs of the almighty

dollar sign – staggers across industry's horizon toward that insanely
biblical light spearing the clouds which might be sunset

or some other big business?

INDUSTRIAL TRINITY

Three squat smokestacks cinched
a little at the waist
will always evoke Three Mile Island.

Each exudes emissions so dense
they linger in the air –
lorgnettes of smog by which

the landscape, regarded
with cool disdain,
is judged and judged upon.

Hills incremental. Farmlands stuttering. Highways strung like spittle.

Commerce is a potent aphrodisiac.

Dream Extraction

The trick is to extract the dream
whole and unbroken, like a squid scooped up in a net.

But like squid, dreams survive poorly in captivity.

Panic-stricken by the change in pressure and atmosphere,
they bang their soft bodies against the sides of the tank
spurting jets of ink until, lost in the cloudbursts of their own alarm,
their hollow bodies collapse in mucilage cave-ins.

For a dream is but membrane fused to motion.
It insists upon the open sequences of sea.

Depth, darkness, and pressure throw open the windows of the skin
through which float vertebrae, ventriloquists, globules of saline.

The trick is to withdraw the dream slowly,
as the spine of a fish is lifted whole
from the snowy parboiled flesh,
a photo-negative.

Then relocate the dream
in an aquarium of semi-permeable glass
through which the dream (a cephalopod)
may pass back and forth, all head and feet,
though it will kick and whimper like a kitten submerged in a sack.

To find the dream, set out slowly through the phosphorescent bay.
Dip your paddle gingerly into water unhurried, where the shape
of ink hangs unbroken, a nationless flag at half-mast.

Don't disrupt the comb jellies that thicken the water,
illuminating the waves at the slightest provocation.

The net of heaven has large holes, yet nothing slips through.
Slip through, rowing softly past the quivering blue lanterns
until everything begins to congeal.

Ignore the distant sirens.
They could be crickets.
Or anything.

Muse Prescriptions

The city gives itself high marks.
"Go easy on yourself," it mutters,
"just lower your standards."
It stares sympathetically into the mirror, plucking its eyebrows.
"Better yet, why not
start taking your meds again?
I really think you need them."

In the East River, both bridges cast long, cylindrical
reflections, green and amber.

Spitting image of –
what?
What else?
Pill bottles.

THINGS I QUESTION

Swedish Cloudberry Preserve?
Fix-a-Dent?
John Boy Walton?
"Live Juice"?
Daylight Savings?
"I'm not racist"?
Inability to quote unquote move on?
Second-class status of animals?
Genetically altered anything?
Future of a bubble?
Cry when I think of you,
Swedish Cloudberry Preserve?

HEAVENS TO MERGATROID!

I have tried to find you, searched for you everywhere
like a sailor whose faith has left him, scanning
the horizon for a familiar star or sign.

In the unmarked grave
between merganser and merge
lies a vacant slot that should by rights define you.

Who or what are you, Mergatroid?

My sole memory of you:
I Love Lucy, the late '50s.
Someone – is it Ethel? – exclaims

"Heavens to Mergatroid!"
which is I guess like saying
"Heavens to Betsy!" or "For Pete's Sake."

It might have been Lucy who said it –
I doubt it was Ricky or Fred –
and while we're at it who in heaven's name

are Pete and Betsy? Mergatroid
sounds like the name of a planet
born of an asteroid or the prime

minister of such a place. A rock
formation, cousin of kryptonite, enemy
of superguys. Like a superguy, did Mergatroid

inhabit only the realm
of sitcoms and cartoons which are themselves
a kind of hereafter?

Just like Miss Mary Mack-Mack-Mack,
Mergatroid died out before having
its day in lexicon court. There is

no mention of Mergatroid
in Webster's Ninth or OED,
no clue as to the he, she,

or it of Mergatroid,
the geology, biology,
or pharmacology of Mergatroid.

Perhaps, like those twentieth-century radio signals
still migrating through the cosmos,
Mergatroid loped quietly off

to heaven, an old mule-god
whose work on Earth was done.
Now, in the blurred esophagus

of outer space, Mergatroid
careens like a capsule pill or spore
waiting to be reabsorbed

in the linguistic gut
of some distant civilization.
Let's hope all language is so resilient

and that somewhere there exists a place
that makes good use
of all we've squandered.

CITY OF SUCHNESS

One night, and then another and another, there were fires.

You said you wanted them,
that you had stood too long
at the shoreline translucent
as a half-sucked lozenge
in a queen's blue throat.

You wanted fires and thin ice to skate on.

Modern life blistered your skin.
Every day the papers said things you couldn't believe:
That Pepsi underwrote the Pope's World Tour.
It's true.

So you swept the news into little channels,
invisible gutters between what you trusted to be true
and what was just too much to know.
The channels swelled into nodules,
luminous and insistent as bobbing lures,
but you refused to bite.

Nights dreamed you unwanted new identities:
narcoleptic in an oxygen bar,
toxified saint nodding out in an alley,
statue of an angel with her wings taped shut.

Mornings woke you thinking different things:
desire to clone yourself so that others might suffer,
catalogue of the insults that have framed your dimensions,
field guide to the miracles you've shunted aside,
those hopeful immigrants forever circling your shoreline
in their splintered boat.

Your telephone rang often. Sometimes you answered it.
"To verify your identity…" the voice once said,
"This will only take a moment of your time."

But you didn't have the time to give,
your American nature worn like perfume behind the ears,
a hurried dab between the breasts, the place
you pledge allegiance,
its essence ever-elsewhere.

Once, in the candlelight of your room,
beneath peeling, centipeded ceilings, you let me hold you.
And for that hour you were calmness in my arms,
your sky a desolate eucalyptus blue, the city
stewing in its own tattoos:
a brief sense of certainty,
ill-founded.

That was before the tick and burn.
Our bones basted in neocolonialism,
hearts callused by advantage.
The rising heat of racism
so distorted the landscape
that everything unfounded glinted alluringly
and everything possible disbursed to a blank radiance
with a half-life of never, endlessly repackaged
to instill the usual brand loyalties.

The temperatures increased as we went about
making and breaking love, burning its humble bridges,
setting even our rivers on fire, the very shoreline,
the boat people whose patient demeanors so inflamed us.

Smoke rose from our reasons, curling
its fingers and toes,

grimacing at the story
America had become, brought to you by
Whomever –
a conglomerate.

We treated our adolescents like toxic waste
and our corporations like children
in need of protection –
spoiled, soft-skulled babies
armed and at the ready.

We gave ourselves over to this vision and did it willingly,
content to fondle a prepackaged future
as promised on the cover of a glossy magazine
to which our subscription, for lack
of payment, had long since expired.

PREDICTIONS

I predict that through a joint venture between PETCO and the U.S. Food and Drug Administration, people will soon be able to clone their dogs and cats in their own homes. The patented process, known as "Perma-pet," will become a national obsession.

I predict a merger between the federal government and AOL Time Warner. I predict that the State of the Union address will be replaced by infomercials for this new mega-entity.

I predict that the United States will change its name to America, Inc.

I predict that in America, Inc., citizens will have to pay for the right to vote.

I predict that corporate sponsorship will become a requirement for citizenship in America, Inc., that everyone will have a corporate logo tattooed on their forehead in exchange for the right to work and that those without such a logo will become untouchables and be forced underground.

I predict that parents will have to register their newborns with their corporate employer in order to obtain a birth certificate and a social security number for their child. I predict that in exchange for citizenship in America, Inc., each child will "belong" to its corporate sponsor – and that biological parents will be viewed as surrogate caregivers whose role it is to raise that child until the time comes to deliver it into the hands of its corporate sponsor.

I predict the word "by-product" will replace the word "child." A world-wide corporate ritual will be observed annually as by-products of the appropriate age group are turned over to their corporate sponsors.

I predict the launching of a prime-time TV program called *Death Row*

Today where executions will be telecast live. I predict that this program will quickly transform itself into a popular pornographic art form.

I predict that Marilyn Monroe's body will be exhumed and that her DNA will be extracted for cloning purposes. I predict the creation of a sexual theme park in Orlando, Florida, composed entirely of Marilyn Monroe clones. I predict that the President of America, Inc. will preside over the theme park's opening ceremonies.

I predict that corporate entities will soon be able to purchase the right to blow up landmarked buildings just as they are now able to buy the right to pollute the air. I predict that the destruction of famous landmarks – the Empire State Building, the Chrysler Building, the Golden Gate Bridge – will become a TV show called *The Rise and Fall...* and that this program will have the highest viewer ratings in television history.

I predict that Ricki Lake will be seen as the Mother Teresa of the twenty-first century.

I predict that Oprah Winfrey will be placed on trial for the crime of promoting literacy in America, Inc.

I predict that the Jerry Springer show and its spin-offs will replace the U.S. judicial system.

I predict that within the next five years, 98% of the American population will be unable to articulate a working definition for the word "privacy."

I predict that the Internet will become the most potent instrument of worldwide social control since the dollar bill.

I predict that McDonald's will become the only legally sanctioned food in America, Inc. Within ten years its corporate headquarters will be based in St. Patrick's Cathedral, and the Egg McMuffin will replace the host during Holy Communion.

I predict that in the wake of a top-secret biotech experiment gone awry, a great bookworm plague will sweep the land. A horde of tiny blue-green beetles will consume all paper and print material: every book, newspaper, photograph, archival record, love letter, and Tampax instruction brochure on the face of the earth.

I predict that this plague will be perceived by many as a righteous act of God and that a worldwide Bookworm Cult will emerge from the wreckage to worship the larval destroyer of print material and the history it carries.

I predict that this religion will dominate Western culture until the end of human time.

(NYC, August 1999)

DEAD CONSTELLATION

Suspended in cocoons of fungal sleep,
we slept

as Privacy was dragged across the sky,
drawn

and quartered by winds North South East & West.
Pity.

She was always such a quiet
girl.

FROM THE ST. AUGUSTINE SONNETS

THIRST

At thy bidding the moments
in the depths
visions attempt us:
forests which keep
ranging   feeding
on the sap upholstery
Is this not how illumination
To whom should we cry?
I am "grass" and thirst
the moments fly
the grass, the stag
Behold the porous spring
Reveal its secrets.
and see. I am "grass"

fly by. Attend us even
attend us with visions [let]
splashed-ink landscape
their stags retired within them –
lying down   ruminating
glistening in the pines.
weeps within us?
Yet my prayer is not for earthly things.
for thee. At thy bidding
by. Despise not
the ruminating range.
of my desire.
Look
and thirst for thee.

PACT

I have told you many things.   21 nights raised
to the sky. Art thou   ignorant? Naked
backside: butter   [   ]
The hours drain   into everything else.
What have   I asked of them?
They jostle me, wolves   of the remaining
darkness. Yet like bones   the hours knit together
first streaks of thy   light.
Temporal. Sexual.   Comfort. [T]error.
I have for a long time been   burning.
Not to take   what is not given.
Yet to give   what is not owed.
Precious to me now   the drops of time.
I offer you the services   of my tongue and mind.

ADMISSION

I wish now to review in memory what could not
be tolerated in life.
Mayest thou grow sweet to me.
Don't say the word. Say it.
I dared grow wild in a succession
of shadowy loves. But you were so vivid, tossing
to and fro. You poured me out. I foamed in
my wickedness, phoned in my love to you, a buck
a minute. All to bridge the hour's indifference
the puddly disturbance between us a voice
from the clouds. I pleased my own eyes, pleased
the sky. What delighted me except to love you
and to be loved? Had only there been something
to regulate my disorder... I wandered still farther into thee.

THY CREATURE

To whom am I narrating?
my world. Your white
My studies interrupted.
did die away from thee.
On whose branches perched
your red creature yours
I will find a way." No signature
unquote. Who falls
In love with thy creature
its bird. My heart
there is no water
And to think for a time I took
thinking not at all, un-thinking.
I didn't see it.

A curtain pulled around
art. A neighboring city.
Until my heart
One leaf. One tree.
a cardinal bruise
truly. "I am water
only a phrase. A quote
from its talons?
the leaf shelters
warns me privately:
no sign of rain.
such pleasure in your exploits
But you doth teach by sorrow.
I rolled in its mire.

The Death & Life of Paul Bowles

I never feel terribly important. I get what I want
or don't. The gentle art of forcing. Pure affection
and unholy desire come on the same blue plate.
Such trouble has the flesh. With the idea of God.
No, no. I never thought of myself as a person. I'm
a recording machine. Ex- cluded from paradise. Going
through life without an idea of God.
I don't think it's a good idea to force it on children
the thought of God.
"So you have no desires?" To what? When I
eat, I'm hungry. When I fuck, I'm horny. When I speak
my mouth is full. Where else could I find such pleasure?
I'm living and soon I'll be dead. *Oh shame*
on you said Gertrude *Anyone can go there.*

Tangier was Gertrude's idea. Alice
said How about Tangier?
Gertrude, dryly: It's constantly hot and sunny.
You'd like it. So there, with tea. "It is good for a man
not to touch a woman." I listened more attentively to words
prayed each time I uncapped my pen, Islamic more
by habitat than belief. Things do seep in. A desert does. Heat
tea and sun the one you really love. A painter.
Sang to his paintings, cross-legged on the floor
imploring their colors to come forth. For which I teased him
mercilessly, the pagan praying to art. As once
I prayed to him. As what is lost   refusing
to believe. As what is lost   refusing to be moved.
An ex-pat is a kind of touch reversed.

A Chance of Snow Later

is predicted by the sign,
but it's snowing now.
Poor Sal Mineo
suspended in lights
above so much weather.
Poor famous dead
and their after-
school specials.
Poor closeted
dead. Snow
now. Snow
later. And
later on,
eons of
aftersnow.

UNTITLED STATIONS

De-escalating wind.
Smoke from the chimney
spells the day's name.
It begins with a T.
All day the day
has been wanting to
snow, yet only pigeons
flurry their similar gray.
Traffic sounds are gone
and bygone. Five blocks
away, the world's largest
cemetery holds its peace.
One has to realize that
the Hours will eventually
have their way –
that's why they travel in gangs.
This feeling fills the streets.
It gouges the window of
Wing's Hand Laundry
with weeping steam.
Hard to believe
how much excludes,
involves us.
Hard to accept that we're just
moments away
from New Year's Day
and that where you are,
it's yesterday, not weeping,
and nowhere near noon.

MR. EGGROLL

Like Zeus you throw the jolt
that turns my head
both ways
slapping mustard
on the sparkly part
of my brain, pink
baloney snow
storm, doom, un-
mistakable cold
splintering candied
branches suckably
smooth & breath-
catching impact
a mouthful
of needles, a thicket
yes pine   yes other
nude branches horse-
shoed   into
silvery spurs
that's me &
you. Xmas
windows half
  splayed behind
numbness of body &
mind, enticing will,
resulting in ever-
greater attachment
to this your world where
rooftops are something
to be worried on
making angels
in snow
competing

with deep snow's
thorough
ornamentation
how plush it makes
the obtrusive city
transforming it
into its own intruder
you know what I mean
the buildings poke
through snow
like slate bouquets
how wrong
it sometimes seems
yet perfect your
face ringed in rabbit
fur   a dense baby halo
when the only open thing
for miles was Chinese
& beneath its star-yellow
MR. EGGROLL
we awaited what
was coming to us
I lay in the snow
on my back for you
waved my arms
slowly & sank
my clock bouquet
deep into
a kind of crushing
that's never really
left me. I still see
you standing above
me, skyscraping. Snow moo
shoo pork & dusk
soft

all of it
soft
a whole night even with
the dozen layers
flammable
synthetic
natural
intrinsic
standing between us
wicking the moisture
from our skins
Hungry Ghosts
immersed
in mess halls
of our own making
in greed & wastage
& the endless
wanting something
else & more.
Hell-beings?
We are them.
Yellow neon
gaseous & elegant
consumed
contained wired &
contained yet bent to the
whim of others.
Or something's
whim. A parent's perhaps,
a famous building
whose idea of greatness
no other structure can erase,
or maybe it's bigger. Can't
answer the question
of why we get on

so poorly
while desire never
goes its separate
way. Sweet-
ness. Beauti-
full hair.
Lone pilgrimage
my thoughts
make through it.
Why is it
we look down on our angels?
Why is it this we need?

GOODBYE MR. CHIPS

Protecting yourself from posterity
you said all the wrong things.
Afraid of Disneyland?
I should certainly hope so.
My name's Petula.
Pompeii's a great place to meet dykes
and lichen. Won't you be my guide?
There's nothing more awful
than being bothered
when you want to be alone.
The steps to my Temple of Jupiter are steep.
Worn like sea air
where the colors avenge themselves
to something like squant.
That's three times already you've made me laugh
my Peter O'Toole
whose eyes are blue
a yellow dress.
Know Thyself:
the watchwords of Apollo.
Tight shot of sky and broken column.
Heterosexual romance the one sure thing
TV sells for free. Once it was considered
a private matter, just ask Joey Know:
we're long past post-
privacy. A rather
repressed lot,
ivy notwithstanding.
But your body is smooth
in your brown silk suit,
you know, the one I bought you
that you now wear for him.
All the curves, the taken aways,

the portions of empty air –
your openings.
Success + $$.
You'll wear it buttoned down.
He'll come extra-close
if only to assert his right to be there.
I won't stand between you.
There's no law against crying.
You must forgive me.
A blurry gypsy at a later table: "See?
The doorway always glitters
as the door slams shut. You're bound
to find someone else."
Oh, Mr. Chips…
You really are…well…Mr. Chips.
Always in character.
A million men with hats.
They're really boys.
Walk slowly and think of cricket.
When we were children – back in China –
we captured them together, even
shared a cage. Home sweet home.
Zombies in the clover.
A choral dungeon.
The crickets are everywhere
conjugating verbs:
Tengo cielo contigo.
So universal.
I carry it with me, the suitcase bigger than I am,
my God I can hardly keep up.
Am I leaving you?
Am I staying?
All I know is I'm going to run.
And write this in my underwear
so my nipples clippity-

clop the keyboard. Don't
worry, it's ergonomic
and so very very blue.
It's what you wanted, isn't it?
The pressure of a poem?
A hamster named Delilah?
An affair that continued, on and
off, for many years?
My sense of timing was dreadful.
I should have said faulty.
For the moment I found you
surprising and civilized.
A sterling intellect.
Why, hello!
I'm looking forward to it enormously.
"Our 15th Anniversary." *Ah*....
I spend half my year in Europe now.
Oh, but why?
My guest of honor, the sparkle
sparkle sea. Under which you sang to me the moon
impersonating a wonderful thing.
At the party, we're supposed to know they're dykes.
This tells us it's decadent.
Theatre people, of course.
You know how *they* are.
The fags and real women are shrill.
Dykes fill the snifters.
An alarm sounds and you move
quickly to another floor.
Therein lies the problem.
But nobody dies.
Don't talk.
I don't want anything to bother you now.
Not even my love.
It must have been what I wanted,

to have been slightly baffled
to have walked that canal.
Anyone could have seen it coming
a mile away. I didn't
choose this loving.
I'm not a part of your world.
Don't go on about it all night long.
See how the glass elongates its dome-ness?
That's how confused I was, how liquidly kissed.
It does not bode well.
A pretty face isn't everything.
You must ask yourself: is she suitable?
That's not even in the dictionary.
They are jealous of the sex of your desire.
A hush falls over them.
The dress so pertinent and yellow.
They can't change an old chap's memory
no matter how they try.
You're not as universal
as you think. Nor am I.
The fireworks have fallen in the river.
God runs a hole right through us.
Yet even now, I won't disgrace you.
Or try to douse you out.
"This person" – they will use the term
advisedly. Something horrible
has happened.
An ultimatum.
It involves some running and some dogs
shrieks and a car and a high-speed chase
a husband, a wife, and a terrible Fall.
Damnificados.
Don't mention it to Apollo.
Not at this eleventh hour.
The first act was Fun.

Act Two: Sheer Misery.
There will be no third.
Such pithy dialogue.
I've come for you.
Don't mention it to Apollo.
He's all out of sympathy.
Bad luck? There's no such thing.
Devilled eggs, anyone?
I loved you bright and perky,
ripe interior
as the iris goes soft.
What an awful lot of flowers.
Cornflowers   ice bars   chocolate
droplets. A fortnight's worth of un-
adulterated joy. Paprika
          violets and eyes.
The water all choked up with lilies. I mean the canal.
A bicycle built for two. But it lies on its side.
It's the last time
we'll take this walk together.
A long, singular road hemmed in by roses,
"a most unpromising premise."
So let's have a toast to it
since it makes us feel grown-up: *the world
has grown a little unlovely.*
Know thyself.
Know thyself.
Blink back the tears.
Oh, don't be an idiot.
Come back.

New Italian Cinema (Napoli Dust)

Since he is living now only with his father, Giovanni is talking in a mysterious language.

A murder in his native town, the accusation of his very best friend, Angelo, an orphan raised by a nomad women.

Old wounds are re-opened and unresolved issues come back to the surface.

In a life filled by obsession, Angela A., a young, beautiful, "obsessive-compulsive" woman, thinks that love can save her and because of that demands love from everyone.

Angela A. and Angela B. (a prostitute) meet in their world where everything comes to pieces and everybody loses something.

Together they'll find the strength and the will to change their life, thanks to their friend and cello player, Roberto.

When his father dies, he is brought before a hospital, then to Volterra by a psychologist and a nurse who wants really to help him.

Colors of the heavenly town. The priest of that town: a local God-father.

A shady French ship owner proposes to Edoardo, a merchant navy captain. Reluctantly, he accepts.

But many problems will occur to him on the way to Bosnia, and he will be forced to make decisions fast.

In the last investigation of Giorgio Nappi, an old public magistrate, close to retire, the Godfather is found guilty, the priest defined innocent.

At the end, everything seems to be solved.

But the old magistrate doesn't stop the investigation of Naples, a city where everything can happen.

WHAT MOVIE NOT TO SEE

Having attained a great age
Fresco sketches
ancient temples
spoiled idols
attached old men
born to be bent
summoned
executed.

One day adoration.
The next, instruction.

Fresco sketches Success
at the time of its destruction –
Success, as it appears to him in his sleep:
burying the sick
visiting the dead.

Sketched in red.
Sketched in red.

PAINT

after a painting by Karen Platt: "Sylvia"

Low art, string theory, the electrical charge
of a demon's horn zooming in on the telephone wire

the unnuanced pink of that early childhood mistake
called *girlhood*. Remix those paints or simply sniff

them, etherize the day. There are no cave paintings
here, no wild bison snorting up the atmosphere,

just canvas skin stretched taut, you know the feeling
and there's a degree of pain involved, a tremendous

amount of pain. At the tip of the brush is a kind of force – not
color – that sucks you right out of your bones like marrow.

I see how it works in you, even now when all you're doing
is *talking* art. It's lodged, every ounce of it, in just one

place. Point to it. Oh, but that's the composition,
is it not? And as far as the woman in the painting goes –

and she might go far – she could be a quiet type or heavy talker,
but she is clearly implicated. Unalloyed. Cadmium. Peligroso

Pink. It's good to make things happen
and to let things stand. To wait and see

without letting that become a form of standing by.
That woman's no innocent bystander.

She's aggrieved.

Transubstantiation

"I feel like a salamander,"
she said, and in
the tall glass
of water on the night
stand she looked
like a red eft
stretched out
in veiled muslin,
something incubating in her pores.

I watched
us touch
in that transforming
realm of water
and glass, a tacky
Vegas mirror
in which our
funhouse bodies
appeared sardonic:

> reduced
> granulated
> extra-kinetic.

As we bent to kiss
or strained upward
to embrace
or reached downward
to restrain

we looked like
sea monkeys
pharaoh hounds
shark fins

tomahawks
leather squid
caryatids
a praying mantis
bouillabaisse.

No wonder our muscles ached
after that strenuous night
in the liquid cylinder,
our night
of being unmade
like history or a bed,
of being reshaped
into a dozen
composite creatures

and then
– exhausting friction –
returned
abruptly
to our skins.

FOR YOU, ANYTHING

Do you like my rubber dress? How about these dentures?
Does the name Steve McQueen mean anything to you?
My favorite word is STREP or SIDESWIPE. My
favorite sentence: *Thar she blows!* Just once,
I'd like to hear someone say to me, *Aye!*
Aye! & act like they mean it. Ein-
stein said, "You cannot solve a
problem with the same mind
that created it." That's
why the sun always
acts on fire & why
outer space likes
to act like
always –
Night.

CLING

All these butterflies and rainy days
headfirst on the branches, aiming orangely upward.
Droplets shine on their wings like sequined scars.
This rain goes beyond punctuation
and almost certainly makes you late.
I'm still trying to make sense of it.
But you're far away, the windows sealed shut.
I once left them open
and the puddles went on for days and days.
I'm trying to believe I have the strength for this,
but strength and strangle are a stone'
sthrow apart, I'm so aware of it now.
I'm willing, yes, but also afraid.
Of what I cannot say.
It doesn't have a handle.
But it's crimped like a wing.

And when I hear the engines starting up
it's hard not to hope you're touching down.
There's so much rain on this runway
yet nothing's really cancelled.
The monarchs take off from the trees regardless,
veering into the dangerous rain with a bright, mottled recklessness –

          as if they really understand this realm
          as if they really mean to take it on.

SOMEWHERE IN WISTCONSIN

There is a River Embarrass.
A tributary, actually.

My problem is

each time I enter the kitchen
I scare those juncos.

They leave pink things
on the outer sill: angulate

                      wentletraps.

To them I want to say:
Don't be afraid,
O cold, inveterate doveliness.

Their flight
yours
and mine –
            simultaneity of melting butter.

Are we really really here? I mean at this juncture.

"You are in my mind always," you say consolingly.

But we don't live inside our minds.

We live in our lives.

FIN DE FIESTA

1: CANDELA

From the candle's vantage point
& waiting. *Freedom from*
your unalloyed absence.
day wish & watch
of a cake decked out
when the varicose lights
of water & motion
The airborne droplets
eardrums to the light.
hearing nothing
& can't be talked out
cake on a platter
the name *"Sincerity"*
crummy

vying for its fulfillment.
are scripted
to roll like sugar

a silent
iridescent scroll. O
Dreams.

? as the crumbs
cascade to the
table.

there are only 2 states: burning
want   wanting   distance
I make this birth-
it sink to the bottom
like bright Niagara
engorge the spectrum
with pure tension.
glisten attentively
They thrum, they thrum
but the beat
of it. Little heart
engraved with veins:
scribbled in icing
little heart

Wishes
in capital letters
from the tongue
a waterfall's barrel
filled with a woman
harbored   dissolving
her life half-lived

Where do they come from
of what's taken

2: CASCADA

I write this to you from behind the waterfall
where everything looks broken. What matters most
does not yell *"Timber!"* It drizzles down.
Don't you wish you could tell the heart
to simply calm without coming to an end?
Even storms must blow their noses. Even thorns
must pierce the crackpot theories of the hours
that make & break their lifelines.
Summer was generous. You were   momentarily
my heart's neighbor our thorns intersecting
like rustic letters aligned against the green.
Don't panic they tried to tell the heart
Don't try to find a reason.
Reason's ash & blocks the stars.

Move through it as a saint headlong
through its halo completely open but not violated.
For a saint, like the heart is an "It"
rushing genderless through the clouds
breaking – not merely bending – gender's unreasoning branches.
As the torso impales the bitter arrow.
As gladness perturbs the more miserable sky.
Behind the waterfall where everything looks broken
gravity takes its stab wounds & re-directs them
toward the stars to grapple with an even steeper
darkness: slow accumulation of these constricting years
ash & thorn & broken branches.
Will they be decades? O how I wish
you'd come around.

3: ESPINA

There are times
as a monk
The room smells holy: talcum
women to whom I play
Simpson licking the handrail
over my head. One whole year
run. Perhaps I was arrogant
I'd made a kind of progress
believing in. A monk's progress
invest in it? I've learned this year
my head bows easily now
the 26 positions on its knees.
makes brief appearances
as I make do

when I see myself
I must stop kissing.
advent   & the moans of good
bridegroom. Like St. Bart
on the IRT, I'm in
boomeranging back at me, a re-
& moved too quickly, thinking
I should probably stop
is a whole new circle. Should I
a brand new set of protocols:
my heart has learned
Even the goddess Anorexia
in her thin white garb
with less & less of you.

4: *LLAMARADA*

Forty waxing sorrows
1 for some future
inclined like the blue-
into her sacrifice:
I walk the aisle
filling my lungs
leaning forward as if
were the flower of an alpine field
vestigial blues. I've never knelt
& properly paid my respects
The list of slim regrets goes on
nodding stems of old flowers
eyes gone to black pollen.
I'm in a high place

blinking on the cake
year   lit & sputtering
&-white striped Virgin
dubious honor of another year.
toward the beckoning light
with annihilating breath
each blurred corona
first blush of spring
in a far-flung meadow
to the blue. Now I've lost you.
each lit to a darkening wick:
after their work is done
My work's just beginning.
the lightning at my side.

5: DHAMMAPADA

In my limited way
you should have left
& come to live with me.
is airborne. *Only the self*
Only the map
This story
We'll let the current
our way across the midst
laughter when
[Page 41: Old Age.]
You wish me memory
Instead, I'm
my wish.
often oddly happy

That my ignorance
is the miracle
as the faucet runs cold.
can shelter
In two years, perhaps
For now, I'm
on the brink of 39:
touched gently
be attentive
this great mass
Like the bee
with its forehead
I gratefully accept
to be free.

of seeing things
[   ]
My trouble
can shelter the self.
revises the landscape.
is not subject to revision.
version stand & wend
of it. *Can there be joy &*
the world is ablaze?
Another birthday comes.
"sin espinas."
without you
But in a good state
lit by little things.

has brought me this far
I press against my temple
Only the self
the self.
I'll come to that page.
in a thorny predicament
Be a good horse
by the whip –
& aware. Put aside
of suffering.
that enters torpor
to the flower
your invitation

GHOST-MATTRESS

I am going back to that half-barren field,
more sand than sagebrush, more trash than land,
going back to those twelve dozen metal cans
all rusted down to an explicit cadmium red,
looking sad, expansive, vaguely pornographic
scattered in the sand of that old impromptu dump.
Don't bother trying to stop me. I know you won't.

I am haunted by that half-barren field
whose prairie dog mounds purse their lips, whistling
circuitous dirges to console themselves in the dark.
Even now, I hear them, urging me back
to find the ghost-mattress.

I came upon it once, far from any landmark,
a long-term resident of the middle of nowhere,
discarded in the field so long ago,
so way, way back, that only its springs remained,
a ghost-mattress with its bone-rows in perfect symmetry,
coiling up from the sand with the same rough, intractable
brightness as red lichen, and the same sense of foreboding.

I am going to wait for nightfall there
amidst the rusting knives and rusted cans of beer
and powder and soda and sardines,
now perforated by corrosion,
now refilled to the lid with sand.
I am going to wait for nightfall in my campfire of rust
while the clouds form a cloud-street in the moonlit sky.
And I know I can count on you
not to come looking.

I am going to spend the night on that ghost-mattress

turning over and over and daring
sleep not to come. My limbs will tangle
in the springs, scraping themselves on rust,
inviting nightmares and tetanus.

All the skittish mammals will emit from their burrows.
The burrowing owls will hop up and down on their mounds,
all face and hunched shoulders, physiognomy of dreams.
All night the aching springs will complain beneath me,
dueling with my sardine flesh.
The cool scent of sage will drift forth
like a faintly mildewed blanket
on an easy summer night.
Surely even you remember that.

The crickets will haul their accordions to the tops of anthills,
risking life and limb for the sake of cabaret.
And the trap-door spiders will listen and wait.

I'll be there, contented at last
amidst the rusting knives and rusted cans
of beer and powder and soda and sardines,
in my impromptu campfire of dust,
watching my aspirations fleck away like rust.

A TROUBLED MIND

When I think of what I could have been –
appliquéing snowflakes to crotchety
branches, carving out cobras
or the Leonine Goddess –

To think
I could have spent my life luring forth the tender light of alabaster,
carrying forth the humid flame of alabaster,
bringing out the very best in alabaster –

I could have been a contender.
I could have been a spelunker.
I could have been a skywriter.
I could have been the winter sky.

My Tumulus

          Something in a ruddy brown,
a softish reddish stone that won't last forever.
I want it low to the ground, an inset. I want
the writing in script and the mention of Brooklyn,
headroom for moss and for those red wingless insects.
Whether I'm actually buried there is of no consequence –
I want only the *idea* of me: brown tablet
set among the owl pellets, jumbo pine
cones, destroying angels – for what is death
but someone else's bright idea?

          A small indentation, like a lapse
or a birdbath, will fill the winter in with
snow and melt with the wild clumsiness
of spring. I want crows to drink there and
cardinals to bathe there, spilling their blood-feathers
for a just and reckless cause. And the blue jays with
their winter extra-blueness
to dip their white stomachs in my cool tureen.

You can lead a horse to water but you cannot make it drink.
I want my tombstone shaped like water for the horses,
a trough for sweet horses,
for when they bring the horses back.

EQUIPOISE

That one time I slept in the stables,
the light from the road nuzzling the beams,
the star-nosed bats in and out all night, squealing –

> In the dream
> everyone just suddenly
> Walked –

> I mean out or away from
> away from it all,
> dropping everything –
>
>> and went off to do
>> whatever seemed
>> realer.

> In the dream
> details didn't matter.

> This was a dream
> of ideals, the actual
> actions invisible,
> as someone said they always are.

> My press pass took me only so far
> into the valley, only so far into
> the dream.

> And at a certain point, I found myself
> turned away.

> At the very last moment,
> someone said, as if to no one in particular,
> "Don't make me explain this to you again."

I woke up
to the heavy sighs and smell
of tethered animals
tethered animals
who stand up while they dream.

LITANY AT DUSK

Let the sky be filled with baroque clouds
encrypted with the last colors of the sun.
Let the orange ones return to me the memory of this same hour
in a different time
when the light stood precisely
as the light stands now: gas station, orange soda, lonely road.
Let those pomegranate torsos turn their ice-nakedness toward me:
heap, billow, buttock, thigh.
Let the mountain infuse itself with sunset, the pink diluted
blood of Christ filling the hypodermic peaks, then draining off
as snowy skin turns blue.
Let fifty-one crows cross the field in a conversational flock.
Let me count them, two by Biblical two.
Let me not forget the one flying solo, a little to the side.
Let the blueberry-stained clouds scud by.
Let daylight clear its cracked white dishes from the field.
Let an insect chitter in the grass like a sugar packet shaken in the ear.
Let the furrows fill with shadows, grape and grape-pigments.
Let a dozen crows fly back the way they came.
Let the two crow communities cry to each other
from opposite ends of the field.
Let their voices meet halfway.
Let them convince each other.
Let the smell of blunt mushrooms instill the air with ether.
Let crisp new shadows aggregate the edges.
Let the earthworms emerge from under the leaf mould.
Let them find each other in the high elevations
of the meadow's damp surface.
Let them scrunch together, mating in the dark.
Let everything melt into an arrhythmia of insects.
Let the magpies call and call and call.
Let the crows repeat themselves one last time,
the starling ventriloquists shut their traps at last.

Let the bulky clouds migrate from purple to purple,
displaying the dorsal fin of the sun's latest gleam.
Let the gibbous moon supervise the setting sun.
Let the darkest clouds drift to more serious darkness.
Let the bone-white clouds encounter them there.
Chalk and Blackboard, erase this day.
Let the bare arthritic branches grow stark against the sky,
cut from black paper   pasted onto this world.
Let the thrumming distant highway seem suddenly near.
Let some tiny creature scurry by, unseen.
Let it not be startled by my presence here.
Let me also go unidentified, unseen.
Let the barbed wire fence go black in its socket,
its sharpness poking through again in slivers of moonlight.
Let the nearest street lamp hum itself to sleep, its green light
pooling on the shiny black road.
Let the road be new. Let it be ready for its pilgrims.
Let the distant dogs bark deeply as if just now coming to.
Let the three-legged Dalmatian run forgetfully across the field.
Let air grow cold.
Fingers grow numb.
Page grow dim.
All but the owls and nightjars grow still.
Let the day's exertions, time, and money pass away.
Even now the clouds carry a frail golden stain.
Let history spread its wrinkled robe, reshuffling its cards.
Let everything yield calmly to the stirrings of nighttime,
its intricate motives,
its immeasurable
manufactures.

CLIMBING YESTERDAY

Ballerina

a hybrid musk
introduced
in '37

seems
most ballerina-
like in late
December
when

her pink
cups crash-
land and

her red hips
(shiny ladybugs)
pirouette

on the tips
of their stems

as compared to
Wing Back Left Garden
blooms

bobbing dejectedly

just beyond
earshot
of some

deliciously
malignant gossip

or sniffling

downcast
at being
subject of same

poor December roses
one might be tempted
to think

poor December roses
beyond the pale

but

winter
hangs back
trellised like

Climbing Yesterday

with just one
dubious bloom
epitomizing

the *idea* of winter
not the deed

and to prove it

here comes
a brite
black and yellow
bee

or bee-like thing
masquerading as
a stingless
                    bee

cheerfully striped
in lacquered
spandex

rummaging
around
the inner sanctum

of one nearly over
snifter plied heavily
with petals

where pollen kings
lie buried
beside their aphid
hounds and
perfumed offerings

reside on
every pew

where the surface
of dying

is precisely
twice
as regal as
the blooming
and oscillates
more brightly

but branches
and vines don't die
well-suited in
armor and
armed with swords
drawn

to discourage
the robins
who nonetheless
nested all spring

among the daggered enclaves
(those nests in late December:
wigs lost in twig-light)

for robins
are too busy
singing
too busy
listening out

for fidgety
earthworms in
burgundy mud

to bother
with barbarous

warnings
nailed up
on vines

robins are
neither brave
nor timid

simply practical-minded

unlike
Arthurian
roses who
in letting down
their guard
are the whole point

of wandering
the December garden
in early evening

inclined
like a tendril

toward blossom
after blossom's
fluctuating light

inhaling the year's
last lemony breath

as the long-held
year exhales

INSIDE THE HOUR

There will first be a rose called Happen-
stance and it will stand in a basket
of stone. Some aren't doing so well,
losing a petal a minute –
twenty moments' worth of ticking,
hard to believe all this
from so little, Proud Flesh.
It would be good to clock
the absolute denuding of a rose,
but every day is different
and what matter are results:
at their feet attention-
grabbing pools of blush and bruise
are scenes of crimes – discarded
pink silk or more mature maroon
gift-wrapped in cirrus ribbons,
the sky in the wake of a long and busy day –
with forty minutes till closing, it marks
its golden errors: cloud pyramid
etch-a-sketched behind some trees.
On the boulder there's a little plaque that reads
This Row Of Trees....
they *are* well-organized, even
from here where the angle's all
wrong. Moving inside me, the kind music
of influence – mine in the world
and that which I've received –
twenty petals of a rose. At least
I hope it's kind.
Like the light on you
which never falters.
The ground is full
of independent businesses –

tiny leaves like red dwarf
stars and countless others,
large   ungainly, who never came near
being stars, curled on their sides
with pieces missing,
crisp brown fists demanding their table.
Something green inevitably intercedes.
A dollar bill. A corset of lawn.
That woman's picking something. It's hard
not to want to. So
when no one's looking…do!
The sound of plucking is the sound
of life – witness waxwings snagging berries.
They sweep the pyramid with
scepter wings, never suspecting its reverence.
Yet the clouds continue
their shimmering twirls
as if candy canes were blue.

A brown bat sallies back and forth
across the cherry   e s   p l a n a d e.

A squirrel trickles down an artery,
a loosening blood clot, formerly
deadly. As in another, playful life
a wave of hands at
top volume: "last rose of summer."
We're long past summer,
how could you fail to notice?
Same as you never see those
nests, now visible
in all their radial splendor,
and the grey ceramic chutes
of paper wasps
like Russian hats of Persian

lambs' wool in the trees.
Pull back the Josephine
Baker rose, sniff
and abandon her.
Push your luck
till the guard pulls up
and says it's time to leave.
A chill adheres. How dull
and thrilling to be a thorn.
But to be a trellis,
now *that's* a life. I'm just not
dutiful enough
to be a rose. Look
at them, the hangers-on,
inspecting the cement
trying to look busy
as they slacken into permanent leaving.
Having once climbed up
they climb back down,
extra-small in
the magnifying lens
of the Brooklyn Museum's
wide brown dome
(upright nipple of a whale).
Like any mammal
they are beseeching,
perhaps for a notebook
named "Roaring Springs"
to journalize their life span.
A trellis, while formal,
is never sufficient, spanning
four ways back into itselfness.
Yet up to a point
it holds things together
like an hour

glass or hour.
Direct light rouses itself
from the garden
a weathered outlaw
on the run, stumbling roughly
back to the territory of some
further westward ho-
ur. It hobbles and curses,
probably drinks too much.
No question it has regrets,
one for every stubbled thorn
it banks its life on, one for
every spur and unclimbed rung.
It is lonesome and encompassing,
but full of slick moves
and never content to stay
in one place for long.
Ah yes, it breaks some hearts.
The guards drive after it
shouting, "The garden is closing! The garden is closing!"
Here's where they start driving really fast and wild
all through this poem.
The garden is closing.
So let it close.

Betsy McCall

Just look at it blooming
a rosy coin
hands and sniffling
is only wind, which
folds average out
moth dips out of.
beneath its pedestal.
rose *Scentsational*
Betsy McCall
Splash? This one's
A poker. Smelling
above everyone
shadow can reach it
Cookie. Sweet

on the top of its game
rising above the grabbing
limbs   the touch that bends it back
always takes what it can get. Its pink
to nearly blue a sphinx
That's the world there, scuffling
Who'd name such a great
when there's Tom Thumb,
Yellow Batman, Splish-
really alive. On a spit.
so personal, a private exchange leaning
and everything. No
so it casts its own: Fortune
Fairy. Mr. Bluebird.

ACKNOWLEDGMENTS

Many thanks to the editors of the following publications where some of these poems first appeared: *asspants* (episode 7), *The Bark online* (www.TheBark.com), *Chelsea, The Fishtank, Frigatezine.com, Gargoyle, The Gay & Lesbian Review/Worldwide, Global City Review, Gulf Coast, The Journal, Pegasus Dreaming, Planet AUTHORity.com, Pleiades, Sojourner,* and *Women's Studies Quarterly.*

I am grateful to the Wurlitzer Foundation in Taos, New Mexico, for a residency in 1999 during which a number of these poems were written. And innumerable thanks to my family, friends, and fellow poets – always, for everything. This book is for Stephanie Gilman, Karen Cook, and Eva Yaa Asantewaa – my Camperdown Elms.